How
Your Body
Works

What Happens
When You

Move?

Jacqui Bailey

PowerKiDS
press™

New York

Published in 2009 by The Rosen Publishing Group Inc.
29 East 21st Street, New York, NY 10010

First Edition

Senior Editor: Jennifer Schofield
Consultant: Dr Patricia Macnair
Designer: Phipps Design
Illustrator: Ian Thompson
Picture Researcher: Kathy Lockley
Proofreader: Susie Brooks

Library of Congress Cataloging-in-Publication Data

Bailey, Jacqui.
  What happens when you move? / Jacqui Bailey. — 1st ed.
    p. cm. — (How your body works)
  Includes index.
  ISBN 978-1-4042-4426-9 (library binding)
  ISBN 978-1-4358-2617-5 (paperback)
  ISBN 978-1-4358-2631-1 (6-pack)
  1. Human locomotion—Juvenile literature. 2. Musculoskeletal system—
Juvenile literature. I. Title.
  QP301.B28 2008
  612.7'6—dc22
                                                    2007041878

Manufactured in China

Picture acknowledgements
Awilli/zefa/Corbis: Cover, 6; Benelux/zefa/Corbis: 25; Goodshoot/Corbis: 7; Martin
Harvey/NHPA: 19b; Jeon Heon-Kyun/epa/Corbis: 14; JLP/Deimos/Corbis: 27;
Kimball Hall/Alamy Images: 12; Clare Marsh/John Birdsall Social Issues Photo
Library: 19T; Medical-on-Line/Alamy Images: 24; Arthur Morris/Corbis: 9;
Oso Media/Alamy Images: 11; Anna Peisl/zefa/Corbis: 23; Reuters/Corbis: 22;
Rick Rickman/New Sport/Corbis: 15; Stefan Schuetz/zefa/Corbis: 26; Holger
Winkler/zefa/Corbis: 20

Contents

How does your body move?

You make thousands of movements every day. You stand up, sit down, twiddle your fingers, and roll your eyes. All these movements can happen only because you have muscles.

When you walk or run, you are moving your whole body from one place to another. When you touch your toes, you are moving part of your body. You choose when to make these movements and you make them on purpose. The muscles that make your body move like this are pulling on your bones.

You can leap in the air, because your muscles pull on bones and make them move.

Some muscles in your body go on moving even when you are asleep.

Sit completely still. Can you feel your chest rising and falling as you breathe in and out? Put the palm of your hand on the middle of your chest. Can you feel your heart beating? Your body makes these movements all the time. You do not usually choose to make them, they just happen. Most of the muscles that make these kinds of movements are moving something inside your body, such as pulling in the air you breathe or pumping your blood around.

Using your brain

Muscles make all the movements in your body, but they need one other thing to make them move—your brain.

Your brain sends messages to your body all through the day and night. The messages travel through long, thin fibers called nerves. Nerves are a little bit like the wires that carry electricity around your home.

The messages tell the muscles when to move. Nerve messages travel very fast, quicker than the blink of an eye.

What is holding you up?

Your body is held up by bones. Without them your body could not move around. It would be just a floppy sack of skin and other parts.

Bones are hard and strong, and they do not bend. They hold up your body in the same way that a set of poles holds up a tent. The set of bones in your body is called a skeleton. Your skeleton is made up of about 206 separate bones, all linked together.

Your skeleton gives your body its shape and helps to protect some of the softer, squishier bits inside you, such as your lungs and brain.

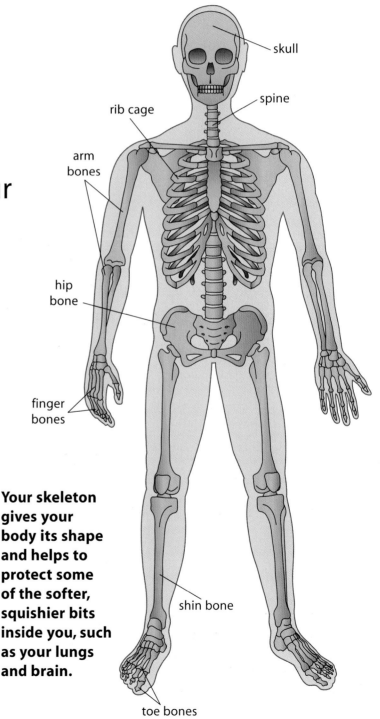

skull

spine

rib cage

arm bones

hip bone

finger bones

shin bone

toe bones

The bones are joined together at the joints. Some bones are locked tightly together at the joints, such as the bones in your skull. These bones do not move. Most joints allow the bones to move up and down or from side to side, or even around in a circle. Think about what happens when you bend your arm. Your elbow is a joint that allows you to bend your arm in half.

Joints allow your bones to move, but something has to stop the bones from slipping and sliding apart. These are the ligaments. They work like strong straps that hold two bones together.

Instead of bones, this crab has a hard shell to protect its body and give it shape. Can you see the joints in its legs, which allow it to move more easily?

On the outside

Lots of animals have skeletons, but they do not all have them on the inside. Some animals have no bones inside their body at all. Instead, they have a hard layer on the outside. Shellfish, such as crabs, wear their skeleton on the outside.

What are muscles?

Muscles work with your bones and joints to keep your body upright and to move it around. Without muscles to pull them into place, your bones would not move at all.

Your body is built out of millions of tiny parts called cells. Different types of cell do different things. Muscle cells are long and thin, like strands of thread, but they are much finer than thread. A single muscle cell is called a muscle fiber. Each muscle is made up of thousands of these fibers grouped together.

You have more than 600 muscles pulling on the bones in your body. Usually, muscles make up about half of the weight of your body.

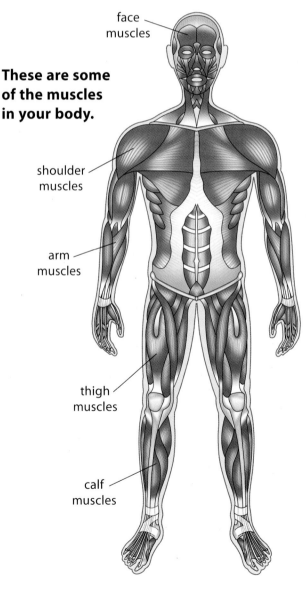

These are some of the muscles in your body.

face muscles

shoulder muscles

arm muscles

thigh muscles

calf muscles

Without muscles you could not stand up, sit down, or wave your arms in the air.

Some of your muscles are large and some are small, depending on where they are and what they do.

The biggest muscle in your body is in your bottom. It helps to move your hips and thighs when you walk or run. The smallest muscle is inside your ear. It is less than $\frac{1}{12}$ in. (2 mm) long—that is shorter than the end of a ballpoint pen.

See for yourself

Meaty muscle

Muscle is the meat wrapped around your bones. Look more closely at a roast chicken drumstick the next time you eat one. The chicken meat on the drumstick is mostly chicken muscle.

11

How do muscles work?

Muscles can work in only one way—they can become shorter, or contract. When a muscle contracts, it gets thicker in the middle and thinner at the ends.

When a muscle attached to a bone contracts, it pulls on the bone and makes it move. When the muscle relaxes, it lengthens out again. The relaxed muscle cannot push the bone back to its original position. Instead, a second muscle has to contract to pull the bone back into place. This is why most muscles work in pairs.

Most of your muscles work in pairs to move your body in thousands of ways.

For example, when you bend and straighten your arm, you use two muscles in your upper arm—the biceps and the triceps. The biceps muscle contracts to pull the lower arm up, while the triceps relaxes and becomes longer. Then the triceps contracts to pull the lower arm back to where it was, and the biceps relaxes and becomes longer.

The biceps and triceps are not the only muscles that move the arm. Other pairs of muscles in the shoulder, lower arm, and wrist all pull in different ways to straighten your arm, lift it above your head, or swing it around. Different pairs of muscles often work together in groups to make your body move in different ways.

Muscle cramps

Sometimes one of your muscles may contract suddenly and you feel a sharp pain called a cramp. Cramps happen most often in the feet or legs, especially if you've been exercising hard. Stretching out the leg or foot as much as possible and gently rubbing it helps the muscle to relax again.

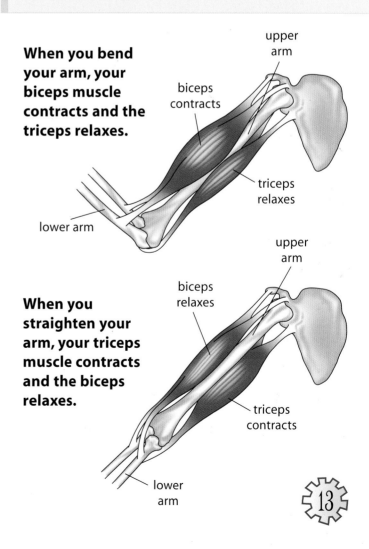

When you bend your arm, your biceps muscle contracts and the triceps relaxes.

upper arm

biceps contracts

triceps relaxes

lower arm

When you straighten your arm, your triceps muscle contracts and the biceps relaxes.

upper arm

biceps relaxes

triceps contracts

lower arm

13

Fixed to bones

In order to pull on a bone and move it, your muscles have to be connected to the bone in some way.

Most muscles are connected to bones by tendons. These are like tough ropes that grow out of the ends of the muscle. They are made from the same kind of material that covers and protects the groups of fibers in muscle. Tendons hold onto a bone by growing into the bone's outer layer, in the same way that plant roots grow into and hold onto the soil.

Some muscles have more than one tendon at their ends. For example, the biceps muscle in your arm has two tendons at the shoulder end, each fixed to a different bone.

Making lots of sudden, sharp movements can injure the tendons in the shoulders, arms, or legs.

14

Tendons are strong and they are firmly fixed to the muscle and bone, but they can be damaged if they are jerked or pulled suddenly. If this happens, the muscles have to be rested until the tendon can repair itself. If the tendon is badly torn, a doctor may have to sew the torn ends together again.

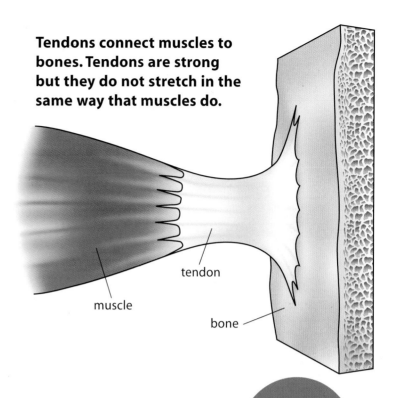

Tendons connect muscles to bones. Tendons are strong but they do not stretch in the same way that muscles do.

muscle

tendon

bone

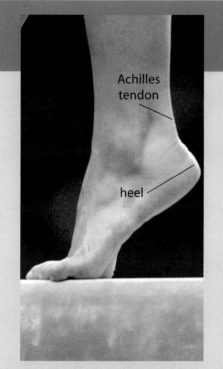

Achilles tendon

heel

See for yourself

High heels

Put your foot flat on the ground. Can you feel the hard, almost bony, strip running from the back of your heel to the muscle at the back of your leg? This is the Achilles tendon. It is the biggest tendon in your body. It pulls your heel up when you walk or when you stand on tiptoe.

On the inside

Not all your muscles pull on bones. Some muscles are attached to other muscles. Many of these muscles move things around inside your body.

The walls of your stomach are made of muscle. So is your esophagus—the tube that leads from your mouth to your stomach—and your intestines—the tube that leads from your stomach to your bottom. When you swallow food, it goes down your throat into the esophagus. The muscles in the esophagus contract and relax one after the other, and this pushes the food until it reaches your stomach.

Muscles move the food you eat through your body from your mouth to your bottom.

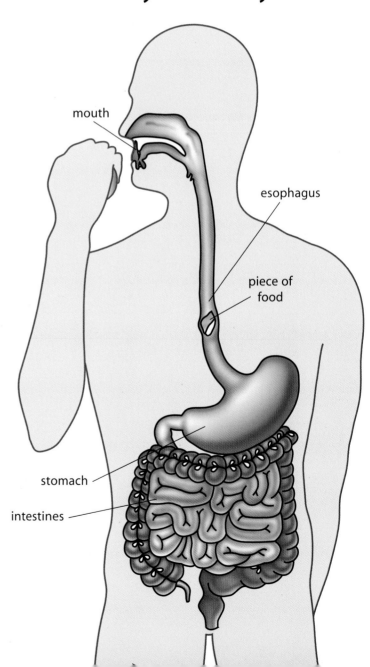

mouth

esophagus

piece of food

stomach

intestines

The muscles in your stomach contract and relax to squeeze and churn the food around and break it up. Then the food is pushed into the intestines. Here, more muscles move it along while the goodness is taken out of it. Eventually, the muscles push any leftover waste out of your bottom when you go to the bathroom.

Your heart is almost entirely made of muscles. It pumps blood by contracting and relaxing every second of your life. Your heart pushes the blood around your body through tubes called blood vessels. These have muscles in their walls that allow them to stretch as blood is pumped through them.

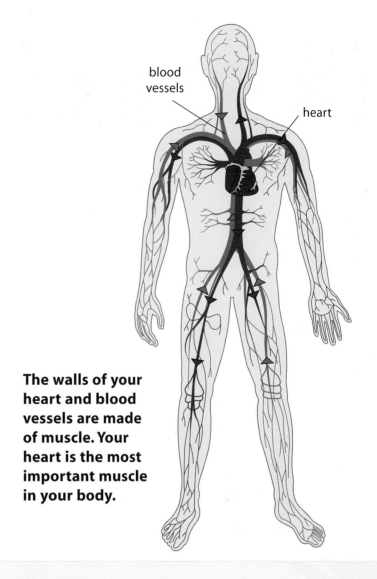

blood vessels

heart

The walls of your heart and blood vessels are made of muscle. Your heart is the most important muscle in your body.

Prickly skin

When you are cold or scared, tiny muscles in your skin contract and pull on the hairs in your skin, making them stand upright. This gives you the shivery feeling we call "goose bumps."

Making faces

You have more muscles in your head and neck than any other animal, except for apes.

Some of the muscles in your head and neck are joined to the bones in your skull, jaw, and spine, but many connect only to each other, or to the skin on your face. These muscles allow you to move your face in hundreds of different ways. You can open and shut your eyes, lift your eyebrows, and open and close your mouth.

You can also use the muscles in your face to show how you are feeling. When you smile, muscles lift the corners of your mouth and eyes, and bunch up your cheeks.

There are more than 30 pairs of muscles in the face. They all work together in different ways to allow us to make hundreds of tiny movements.

Humans use the muscles in their faces to send messages to each other. Can you tell what these faces are saying?

When you frown, other muscles pull the corners of your mouth down, lower your eyebrows, and wrinkle your forehead.

You also use the muscles in your face to bite and chew. Muscles pull on the jaw bones in your mouth, opening and closing your lower jaw. Other muscles in your cheeks help to move food around in your mouth as you chew. The muscle that clamps your jaws together when you bite is one of the strongest muscles in your body.

Familiar faces

Most animals do not have enough muscles in their face to show any emotions. Only apes, such as gorillas and chimpanzees, can move their faces in as many ways as we can, and use these movements to show their feelings.

Making sounds

Every time you speak or make a sound, you are using different muscles.

You need air to make sounds, and you need muscles to get air. When you breathe, you use the muscles between your ribs and the large sheet of muscle, the diaphragm, that sits below your ribs. When these muscles contract, air is pulled into your lungs. When they relax, air is pushed out of your lungs.

When you breathe in, air travels from your nose or mouth down a tube called the windpipe and into your lungs. As you breathe out, air travels back in the opposite direction. Inside your windpipe is a voice box with two folds of skin, called vocal cords. Muscles in your voice box make the vocal cords open and close very quickly, so that air passing through them makes a sound.

Women's vocal cords move twice as fast as men's, which is why their voices are higher.

As air moves through your voice box, your vocal cords open and close very quickly to make sounds.

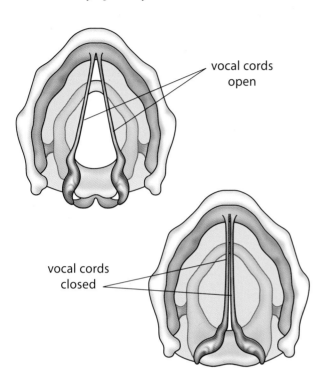

vocal cords open

vocal cords closed

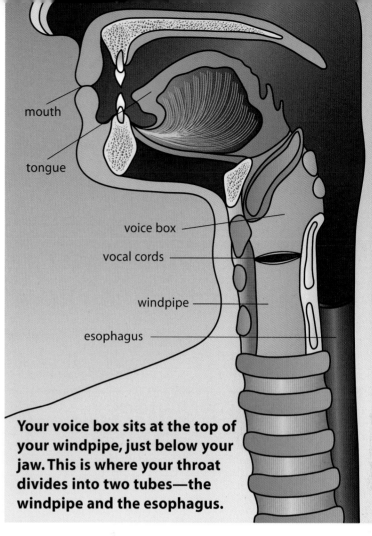

mouth

tongue

voice box

vocal cords

windpipe

esophagus

Your voice box sits at the top of your windpipe, just below your jaw. This is where your throat divides into two tubes—the windpipe and the esophagus.

As sounds travel up your throat and out of your mouth, you shape them into laughter, songs, and speech by moving lots of small muscles in your tongue and lips. Try saying something without moving your tongue or your lips—it is very difficult!

Tongue twister

The tongue is the most bendable muscle in your body. It can twist and turn in almost every direction. In fact, the tongue is not just one muscle but lots of muscles, all overlapping and working together. It is also longer than it looks. An adult's tongue is about 4 in. (10 cm) long.

Being active

You cannot make new muscles, but you can keep those you have healthy and strong by exercising them regularly.

The more your muscles move, the better they work. This means you can use them for longer before they get tired. When muscles are not used, they become weak and lose their shape. Your bones also weaken and your joints become stiff and do not move so easily.

Exercise is important for healthy bones and muscles, but you can damage them by doing too much exercise too suddenly, or by doing the wrong kind of exercise.

Body builders make their muscles bigger by lifting heavy weights. If you lift weights before you are an adult, you can damage the way your muscles and bones grow.

22

Yoga and gymnastics are both fantastic ways to keep your body supple.

Athletes can injure themselves if they work their bodies too hard. Sports that need lots of strength have to be started slowly and with proper training. For example, long-distance runners have to train their muscles to work steadily over a long time. They do this by slowly increasing the distance they run. Tennis players do a mixture of exercises to allow them to use short bursts of strength and lots of joint movements as they sprint, leap, and stretch for the ball.

Warming up

Never do any sport or exercise without warming up your muscles a little first. Warm-up exercises use gentle bending and stretching. When muscles move, they use up energy and give out heat. Warm muscles contract and relax more easily and are less likely to be injured.

Breaks and sprains

Bones are strong and hard wearing, but they can crack and break if too much weight is suddenly put on them, or if they are hit by something hard.

Cracks or breaks in bones are called fractures and they are very painful. Bones are amazing, because if they break, they will usually repair themselves. The bones make new bone cells that grow over the broken ends and join them back together.

To help a bone heal properly, doctors make sure it is straight and the broken ends are in the right position.

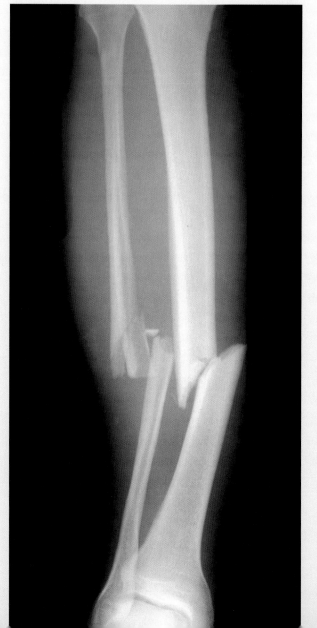

This X ray of the lower part of the leg shows that both bones have been broken.

24

Wearing pads on your knees, elbows, and hands when you are doing some sports helps to protect your body from cuts and grazes, as well as from fractured bones.

Sometimes doctors wrap up a broken arm or leg in special bandages that set into a hard cast or shell. This fixes the bone in the right position while it is healing. It can take months for a broken bone to grow back together.

Ligaments, tendons, and muscles can also tear. A torn ligament is called a sprain. A torn tendon or muscle is called a strain. Sprains and strains can happen when people fall and jerk, or twist a part of their body awkwardly, or do too much exercise too suddenly. Both types of injury usually heal themselves, as long as the injured part is not used for a while.

Bone protectors

Breaks often happen when you are moving fast and fall or crash into something. The best way to protect yourself is to wear a safety helmet and elbow, knee, or ankle pads when you are Rollerblading or skateboarding.

Looking after your bones and muscles

Like all the parts of your body, your bones and muscles need a good supply of oxygen and food to work properly.

Oxygen is in the air you breathe. Your blood carries oxygen from your lungs to the cells in your bones and muscles. Your cells use oxygen to get energy from food. Cells need energy to grow and repair themselves, and to do whatever it is they are needed to do.

Exercise strengthens your heart muscle. This is important, because the heart pumps food and oxygen to the rest of your body.

A mineral called calcium is very good for your bones, especially when you are young. Milk, cheese, and yoghurt contain lots of calcium.

Muscles use up lots of energy, and the harder they work, the more energy and oxygen they need. Being active makes you breathe faster and more deeply, and brings more oxygen into your body. Regular exercise trains your lungs to take in more oxygen. It also makes your muscles stronger.

As well as giving you energy, food contains chemicals called vitamins and minerals. Muscles and bones need small amounts of these chemicals every day to keep them healthy.

Some foods, such as vegetables and fruit, have more vitamins and minerals than others, especially when you eat them raw. Other foods, such as meat, fish, eggs, nuts, and beans, help your body to build up and repair muscles.

Growing up

As you grow from a baby to an adult, your body gets taller. This is because your bones grow longer. Some time between the ages of 15 and 20, your bones stop growing and after this you will not get any taller. You will have reached the right height for your body.

Body words

Words shown in italics, *like this*, are a guide to how a particular word sounds.

Biceps *(bye-seps)*
The muscle in the front of your upper arm.

Blood vessels
The network of tubes that carry blood to every part of your body. Blood vessels include arteries, veins, and capillaries.

Cells
Tiny bits of living material from which all of the parts of your body are built. There are lots of different types of cell in your body—most cells are much too small to be seen without a microscope.

Diaphragm *(dye-uh-fram)*
A thick shelf of muscle that lies under your ribs, between your lungs and stomach.

Esophagus *(uh-sof-fuh-gus)*
The stretchy tube that carries food from your mouth to your stomach.

Fracture
A break or crack in a bone.

Intestines
A very long, stretchy tube leading from your stomach to your bottom. The intestines is folded up to fit underneath your stomach. It has two parts: the small intestine and the large intestine.

Joints
The places where two bones meet. Joints allow the bones to move. The knee joint lets you bend the middle of your leg, for example.

Ligaments
Strong fibers that hold two bones together at a joint.

Muscle fibers
The types of cell that make muscle.

Nerves
The types of cell that carry messages between your brain and the rest of your body. Nerves tell your muscles when to contract and relax.

Skeleton
All the separate bones in your body, grouped together.

Sprain
A damaged or torn ligament.

Strain
A damaged or torn muscle or tendon.

Tendons
Strong, ropelike fibers that connect muscles to bones.

Triceps *(try-seps)*
The muscle in the back of your upper arm.

Vocal cords
The folds in your throat that use air to make sounds. You shape the sounds you make by moving different parts of your mouth and throat.

Voice box
The part of your throat that contains your vocal cords.

Windpipe
The tube that leads from the back of your nose and mouth to your lungs.

Body facts

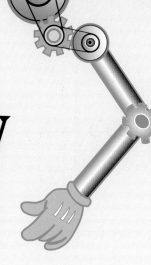

- Millions of nerve messages travel between your brain and your muscles every second.

- You were born with more than 300 bones, but some of these bones grew together as you got older.

- A single muscle fiber can be up to 12 in. (30 cm) long.

- Women have high voices because their vocal cords open and close more than 200 times a second.

- The busiest muscles in your body are the ones that move your eyes. Your eyes make millions of small movements every day.

Index

Web Sites

Due to the changing nature of Internet links, PowerKids Press has developed an online list of Web Sites related to the subject of this book. This site is updated regularly. Please use this link to access this list:
www.powerkidslinks.com/body/move